Fighting Disease

by Michelle Hyde Parsons

Table of Contents

You have a fever. You have a cough. You can have a **disease**.

How do you get a disease? How can you fight disease? Read this book to learn about disease.

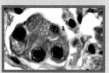

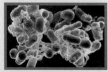

What Is a Disease?

A disease is something in your body. A disease makes you feel sick. Your body does not work well.

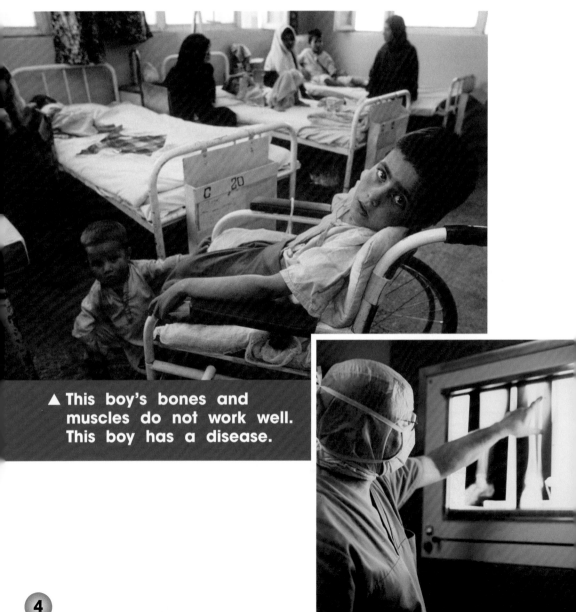

▲ This boy's bones and muscles do not work well. This boy has a disease.

You can feel sick when you have a disease. You can feel tired. You can have pain. You can have a fever. Feeling sick and tired are **symptoms** of a disease. Pain and fever are symptoms.

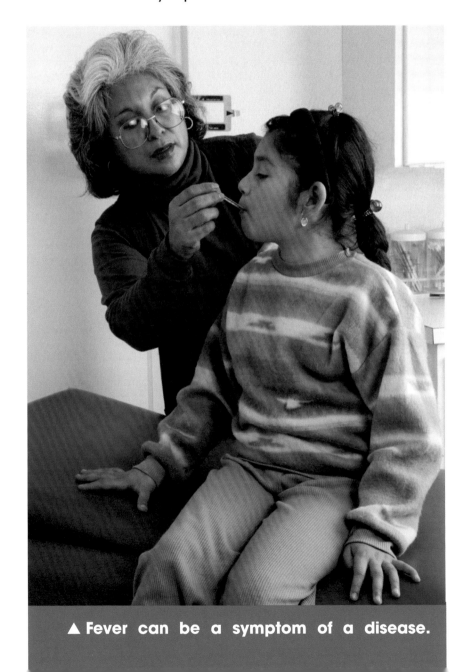

▲ Fever can be a symptom of a disease.

Many things can cause disease. Dust and mold can cause disease.

Sometimes a disease is serious. Sometimes a disease is not serious. Some people have asthma. Asthma is a disease.

▲ **Dust and mold can cause asthma.**

Did You Know?

Plants can cause disease. A poison ivy plant caused this skin disease.

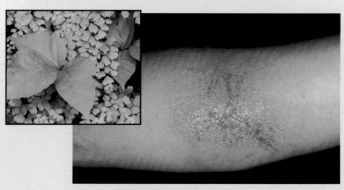

▲ **A poison ivy plant caused this skin disease.**

Germs can cause disease. **Viruses** and **bacteria** are germs.

Diseases From Germs

Disease	Cause	Symptoms
Chicken pox	bacteria	runny nose, cough, red spots
Influenza (flu)	virus	fever, body aches
Pneumonia	bacteria	fever, chills, chest pain
Measles	virus	red spots on skin
Tuberculosis	bacteria	cough, fever, chest pain

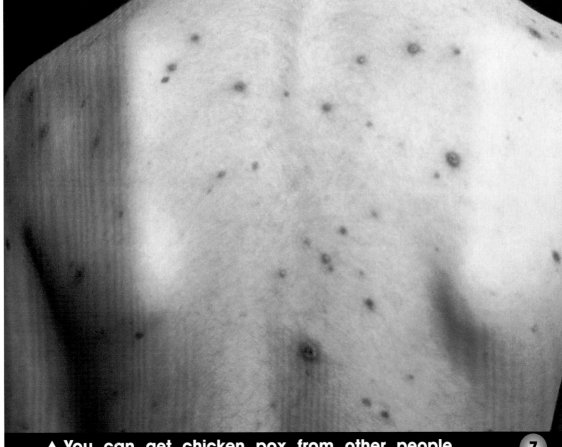

▲ **You can get chicken pox from other people. The bacteria travels in the air.**

What Do Viruses and Bacteria Do?

A virus is a germ. A virus causes disease. A virus cannot survive alone. A virus needs a **host**. A person can be a host to a virus. You can be a host to a virus.

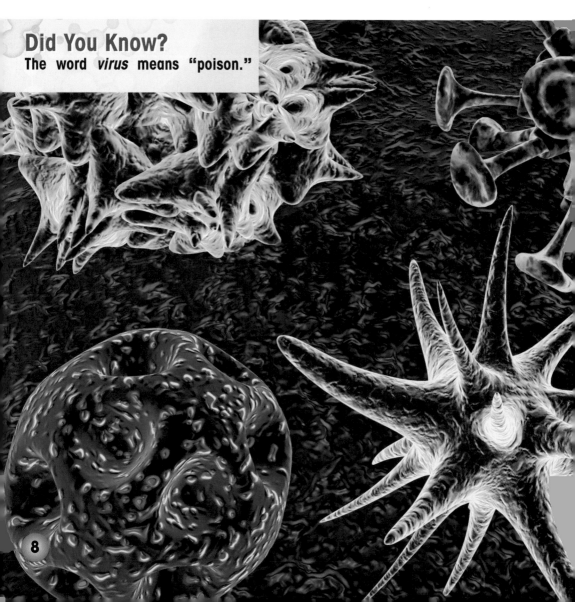

Did You Know?
The word *virus* means "poison."

8

A virus can enter your body through your nose. A virus can enter your body through your mouth. A virus can enter your body through a cut.

It's A Fact

A person with a virus sneezes. The virus moves to another person. Now two people have the virus.

▲ Viruses have different shapes.

Your body is made of **cells**. A virus can enter some of your cells. The virus uses your cells as food. The virus makes another virus. Then the virus is very strong. Now the virus can kill your cells.

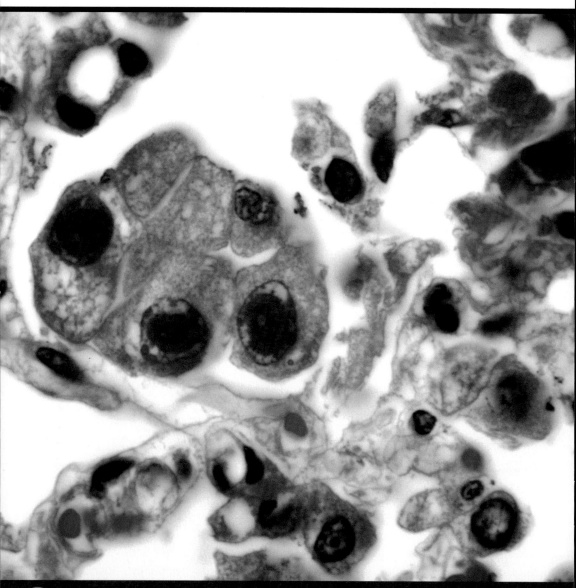

▲ A virus uses your cells to make another virus.

Bacteria are germs. Bacteria are tiny cells. Bacteria can move. Bacteria eat healthy cells. Some bacteria eat other bacteria.

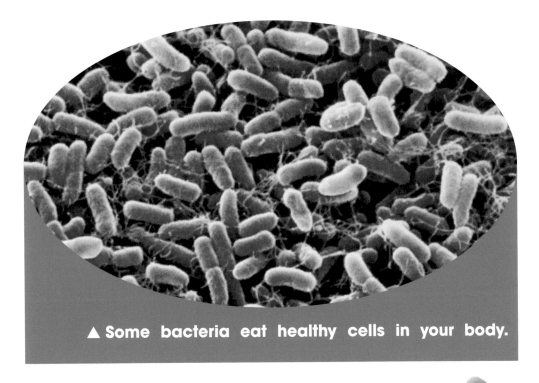

▲ Some bacteria eat healthy cells in your body.

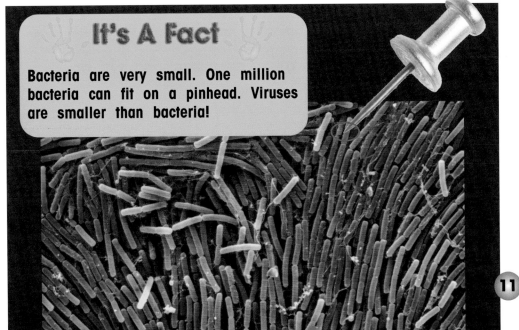

It's A Fact

Bacteria are very small. One million bacteria can fit on a pinhead. Viruses are smaller than bacteria!

Bacteria create **waste**. The waste kills healthy cells. Then people get sick.

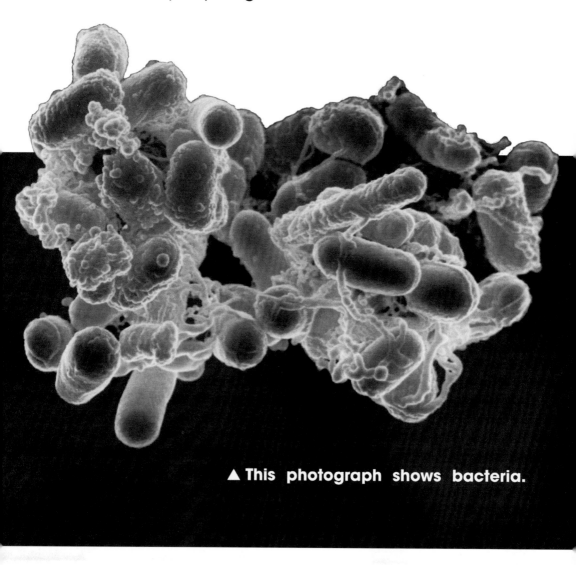

▲ This photograph shows bacteria.

It's A Fact

Some bacteria are good for you. Some bacteria kill viruses. Some bacteria help you digest your food.

Bacteria and viruses are everywhere. Bacteria and viruses are in the air. Bacteria and viruses are in food. Bacteria and viruses are in water. Bacteria and viruses are on things you touch.

How Does Your Body Fight Disease?

Skin helps your body fight disease. Skin helps keep germs out of your body. Nose hairs help your body fight disease. Nose hairs help keep some germs out of your body.

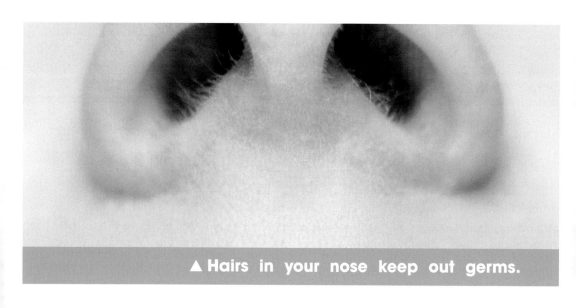

▲ Hairs in your nose keep out germs.

Did You Know?
Nose hairs keep small insects out of your body.

Saliva is the liquid in your mouth. Saliva helps your body fight disease. Saliva can keep out germs.

Acid in your stomach kills germs. Your tears can wash away germs.

▲ Tears wash away germs.

Did You Know?
Some scientists think elephants cry.

Your **immune system** helps your body fight disease. White blood cells are in your immune system. **Antibodies** are in your immune system.

It's A Fact

Leukemia is a disease. Leukemia is a type of cancer. Leukemia makes too many white blood cells.

▲ White blood cells are part of your immune system.

The white blood cells travel through your body. The antibodies travel through your body. The antibodies attack germs.

▲ Antibodies are part of your immune system.

What Can Help Your Body Fight Disease?

Healthy bodies can fight disease. Strong immune systems fight disease. How can you have a healthy body? How can you have a strong immune system?

Sleep helps you have a healthy body. Sleep lets the body rest. Rest helps the immune system stay strong.

▲ Sleep helps you fight disease.

How Can You Sleep Well?

1. Stop watching TV at least one hour before bedtime.
2. Stop exercising at least one hour before bedtime.
3. Stop eating at least one hour before bedtime.

Healthy foods help you have a healthy body. Healthy foods help your immune system stay strong. Do you eat healthy foods?

Try This

Write down all the foods you eat for a week. Are you eating healthy foods?

▲ Healthy foods help you fight diseases.

The diagram shows healthy foods. The diagram shows different types of healthy foods.

Solve This

Look at the food diagram. Which foods should you eat the least? Which foods should you eat more often?

Grains   Vegetables   Fruit   Milk   Meat & Beans

Exercise helps you have a healthy body.
Exercise helps your immune system stay strong.
Then your immune system can fight disease.

▲ Yoga is exercise.

Walking is a type of exercise. Running is a type of exercise. Swimming is a type of exercise. What types of exercise do you do?

▲ **Swimming is exercise.**

Washing your hands helps you fight disease. Washing your hands washes away germs. Then the germs cannot get in your body. Do you wash your hands?

▲ **Washing your hands helps you stay healthy.**

Medicine helps you fight disease. Medicine kills bacteria in your body.

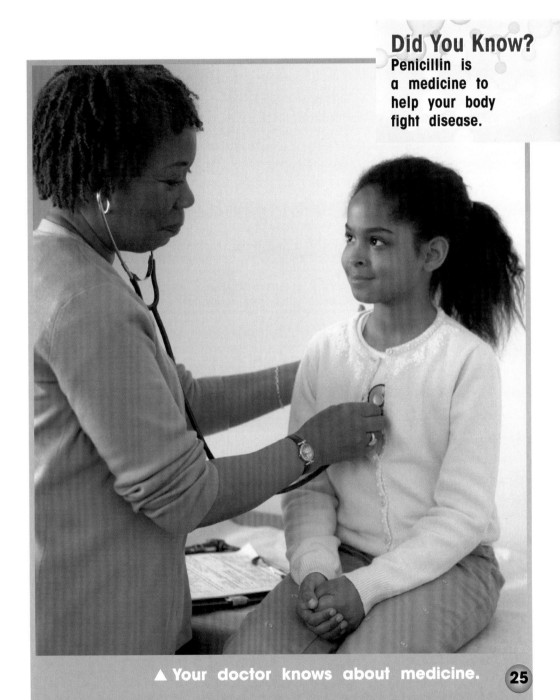

Did You Know?
Penicillin is a medicine to help your body fight disease.

▲ **Your doctor knows about medicine.**

Germs are all around you. Germs are in the air. Germs are on the things you touch.

▲ You can fight disease by staying healthy.

You can help your body fight disease. You can help your body fight germs. You can help your body stay healthy.

It's A Fact

Flu shots help protect you from the flu.

Viruses and bacteria cause disease. Your body fights disease. You can help your body fight disease in many ways.

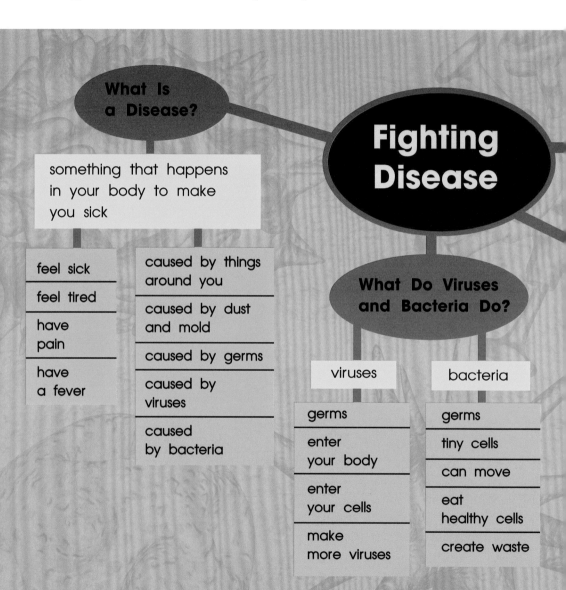

What Is a Disease?

something that happens in your body to make you sick

feel sick
feel tired
have pain
have a fever

caused by things around you
caused by dust and mold
caused by germs
caused by viruses
caused by bacteria

Fighting Disease

What Do Viruses and Bacteria Do?

viruses

germs
enter your body
enter your cells
make more viruses

bacteria

germs
tiny cells
can move
eat healthy cells
create waste

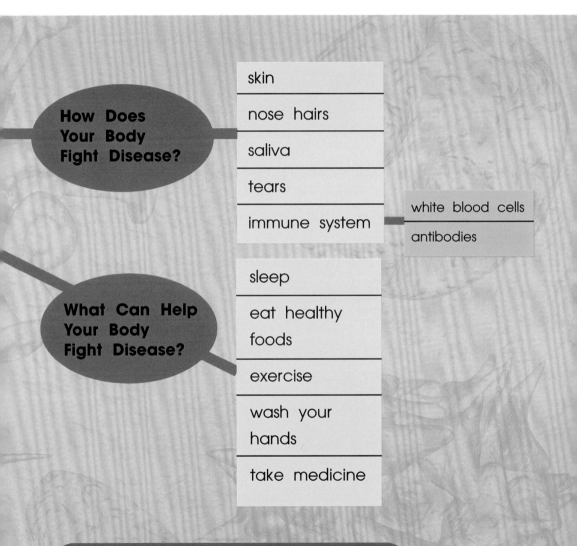

How Does Your Body Fight Disease?

- skin
- nose hairs
- saliva
- tears
- immune system
  - white blood cells
  - antibodies

What Can Help Your Body Fight Disease?

- sleep
- eat healthy foods
- exercise
- wash your hands
- take medicine

Think About It

1. How do viruses cause disease?
2. How do bacteria cause disease?
3. What can you do to fight disease?

antibodies things your body produces to fight germs

*Your immune system has **antibodies**.*

bacteria one-celled germs that cause disease

***Bacteria** are germs.*

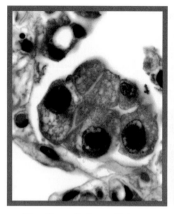

cells tiny living things that make up your body

*Your body has millions of **cells**.*

disease sickness

*Asthma is a **disease**.*

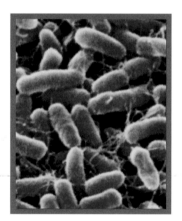

germs bacteria and viruses

***Germs** cause disease.*

host a person in which a bacteria or virus lives

*You can be a **host** to a virus.*

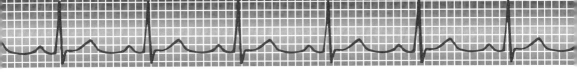

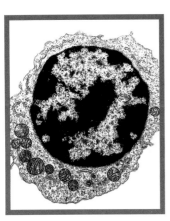

immune system parts of the body that fight disease

*Your skin is part of your **immune system**.*

symptoms signs that you may have a disease

*Fever and feeling tired are **symptoms** of disease.*

viruses small germs that cause disease

Viruses can cause disease.

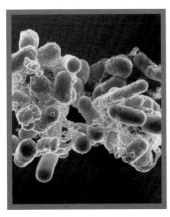

waste something that is unwanted or cannot be used

*Bacteria **waste** kills healthy cells.*

Index